ADIEU PLANE SNAKE

First edition, June 2025.

ISBN-13: 978-1-939502-49-0

Published by Penciled In

5319 Barrenda Ave

Atascadero, CA 93422

penciledin.com

Book interior design by Benjamin Daniel Lawless.

Cover art was designed by Benjamin Daniel Lawless, and includes these public domain works:

- Fasciated snake or Blue snake or wampum snake illustration from The Naturalist's Miscellany (1789-1813) by George Shaw (1751-1813).
- Plane. Photo Courtesy of Royal Norwegian Navy. Original public domain image from Flickr.

Interior photos all by Benjamin Daniel Lawless, using different models of iPhone over the years.

This book was designed and laid out using Affinity Publisher 2.6.3 on a 2024 Mac Mini M4 running macOS Sequoia 15.5.

Other books by Benjamin Daniel Lawless:

- *The Last Spelling Bee*
- *There is Nothing Poetic About Fish*

ADIEU PLANE SNAKE

Five-letter Words That Create Accidental Poems

Brought to you by

Benjamin Daniel Lawless

For my mom, who taught me

to point at the magic

in the mundane.

Introduction

Wordle has been an obsession and a fun way to compete with my family and friends, even when we were apart. At around 8 am on January 27, 2024, something strange happened.

08:08
99
Wordle
Subscribe to Games
A D I E U
P L A N E
S N A K E
Q W E R T Y U I O P
A S D F G H J K L
ENTER Z X C V B N M
AA
nytimes.com

I shook my head. "ADIEU PLANE SNAKE" felt bigger than the sum of its words.

It was Samuel L. Jackson shouting about opening a window in *Snakes on a Plane*. It was brazen. It was funny. How could this be? A screenshot must be taken.

Many mornings, after I blearily enter these strange five letter words, meaning appears. This usually happens before coffee.

Screenshot. Save. Eventually, a collection formed.

POWER STARE CURSE

GROAN WHILE FUMES DEBUT

CRASH SMASH STASH

FOUND LIARS BEACH

DOING RAMPS SMART SCRAM

IRATE INANE IMAGE

Wordle limits you to five letters, yes, but it also has another interesting feature that is divorced from most poetry forms: if you get a letter right, it stays in that spot for future words. This is completely at odds with crafting verse, yes? And yet, there's something profound here.

How Wordle works

- The game selects a five-letter word for the world to guess. These words are typically common nouns. Everyone who plays on that day guesses the same word.
- Players input a guess by typing in their own five-letter word.

- After submitting a guess, players receive visual cues based on the accuracy of their guess:
    - If a letter is highlighted in green (or orange in high-contrast mode), this indicates that the letter is in the correct position within the target word.
    - If a letter turns yellow (or blue in high-contrast mode), it signifies that the letter exists within the word but is in the wrong position.
    - A gray tile indicates that the letter is not present in the target word at all.

- Players only have six attempts before the game ends. If you lose, you can't play any more that day.

LIONS PARTY CREEK CHEER

HOUSE COOLY LOCAL

ABHOR CLOSE CLONE

AMIDS AUDIO ABIDE

ORGAN WRONG BINGO DINGO

Perhaps we are just the vehicles by which we process all of life: the universe splatting spaghetti against our attention.

Our minds are hungry to process patterns, and thus these completely unintelligible sequences build their own meaning.

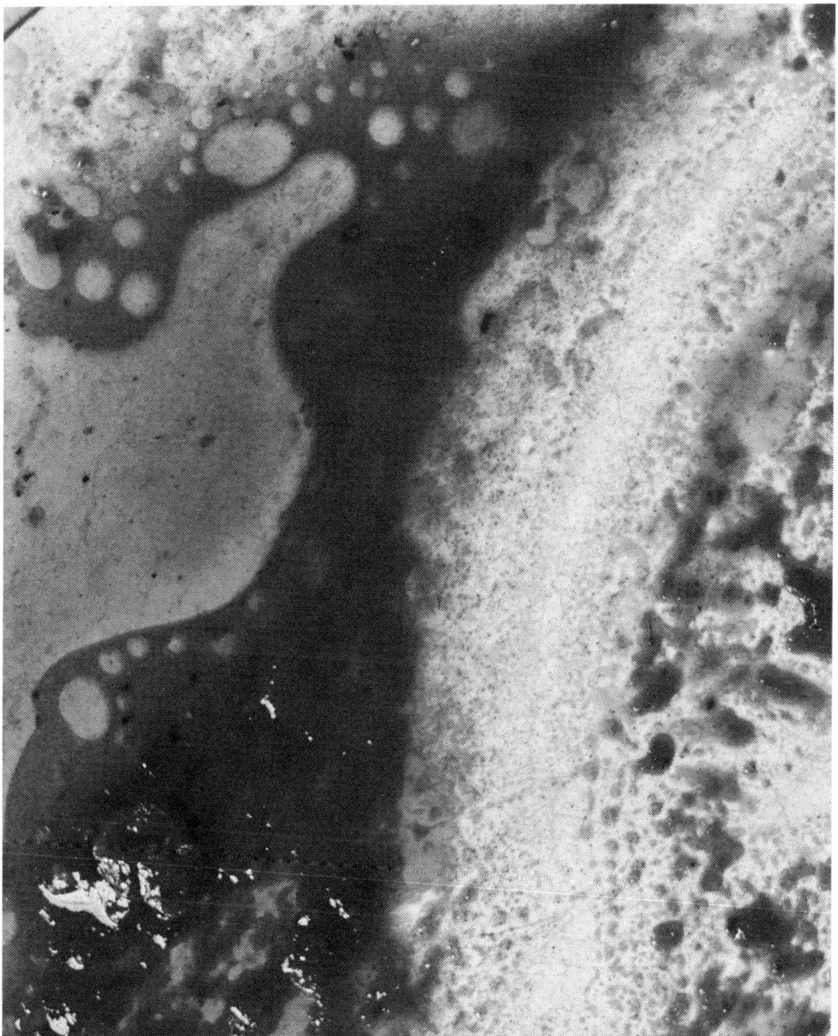

SINCE TOUCH TORCH

ARSED LASER

HOURS RELAX REPEL REVEL REBEL

PHASE ALONG ARMOR ARROW

GHOUL GUIDE GUMMY

FLINT POSED SMOCK CHAOS

I find that art can be defined as pointing at something that is noticed.

As important as creation is, art owes much to the curation, the presentation, and the reception of the work.

PLANTER?

FLUTE TREES EVENT

QUOTE SMILE BROKE OZONE

GHOUL SPILL PEARL EXPEL

LOOKY LEADS LITHE

LEAST FAIRY ARROW

GROAN ORGAN

PEARL ELFIN FILET

FRIED GHOUL SNOUT SPOUT

UNDER NIGHT POINT SAINT FAINT

Another strange feature of this practice is the lack of punctuation.

In design courses, I learned about the principle of gestalt. It has to do with the way your brain recognizes and completes a pattern.

My mind has filled in the punctuation in these, but perhaps your mind has placed the punctuation elsewhere. Gestalt gestating in the guesses.

EARLY IN THE SOLAR REALM

YOUNG HEART SKATE

SALTY STORE STOOD

FRIED ROAST ROACH

POUTY TRIED LATCH STALL

BEACH TRIES OWLET OFTEN

TRASH LACKS

LEARY OF OUTER ROUTE

There are so many delicious five letter words.

There's nothing better than LUNCH. Or MEALS. Even BAGEL.

To get good at Wordle, you may want to start with words with the most unique vowels, like ADIEU or AMIGO.

To get good at uncovering these poems, you may choose to start with words you don't regularly use. Perhaps an object or a subject that you can follow with a five-letter verb?

CLOWN CROWN

TRUST CARPE READY

BREAD CREAM TREAT FREAK

YACHT CLAIM SCALE

LEARN BRAKE BRACE

FRIED POUTY PLANT STAMP

CRASH BRINK BRING BRINY

A note to time travelers: you are more than welcome to use my poems to cheat at Wordle's past.

Contact me, prove you are a visitor to our time, and I will provide you with the dates for each of these poems.

Success is yours for the taking.

SAUTE FLARE GLAZE PLACE

TREAD LIGHT BUILT FLINT

SHEAR RELIC FRIED

TRIPE TARDY TURNS TURBO

ADIOS CHORE BROTH

MONKS SHUCK STEAK SPARK

ROUTE TREAD AFTER EATER

In a couple of places, I have cheated for my own creative purposes.

I haven't added any main words (maybe a couple of interstitial words, denoted by not being in caps), but I did remove a few. In very select places, I reordered words.

I consider this my privilege as this is my book.

Nanner nanner.

Write your own.

GREAT BRAIL CRAWL

HOUSE LEARN REALM

MOUTH FLOWS GROWL PROWL

SHAPE SLEEK STEEL

HYPER THINK MOUTH MATCH

CHIMP SPEAR PREYS

Sometimes the Wordle isn't enough.

Maybe you'd like to use the words to make a

"more legitimate" poem?

AUDIO BLAME PARTY PANTS PASTA

Audio from upstairs shakes the block

And me? A concerned neighbor

ready to pin blame.

Knock knock.

Sure, I expected a party,

but why is that man

wearing pants

made of pasta?

LAUGH AFTER CRAFT DRAFT

& FLOWER AFTER SAFER WAFER

LEARN FLASH SLASH CLASH

LIVEN DEATH SHADE

POWER LEACH CHAFE CHASE

SHARE CLOVE

BLIND BLITZ BLISS

This book was compiled from over 90 screenshots.

It was gathered for a poetry performance on June 29, 2025 at Studios in the Park in Paso Robles, California. This performance is intended to have accompaniment. I asked musicians I know to play music with my performance and they declined*, so I thought "What about the accompaniment that can be made during the creation process?"

What if my accompaniment was Wordle?

Am I allowed to make something so irreverent, so completely potentially devoid of artistic merit? Well, it's my book, and you're reading it. Thank you, and you're welcome.

* *My son, when asked to play ukulele or drums in front of a crowd to my poetry, said "ABSOLUTELY NOT." And how can I blame him? Other musically-inclined friends had similar, if not as harsh or terse, responses.*

LYING TROUT TUTOR

ARIEL MUSIC TOXIN

GLOAT LIVEN BELLY JELLY

FREAK BRICK CROOK

GREAT SEVEN MELON

&

GREAT SLIMY BUDDY

&

GREAT FOUND FUNKY REPOS

CHORE FORCE

These poem-puzzles sprouted starting January 27, 2024

and the last one I've collected in this volume is from April 29, 2025.

In that time, the western world and our interior world has shifted significantly. May you find peace in an ever uncertain landscape.

Check the back of the book for a way to see even more poems like this, and even to contribute your own.

PARTY MINTY DITTY

MOUND FLUNG FLUNK

MOUSE BOAST

&

GHOUL SHOUT

SADLY GRAMP THANK KNAVE

SERUM SLEEP SPECK

If anybody says you are not enough, pay no mind.

All advice is autobiographical, and so is criticism.

I'm here to tell you: you are enough. Your mirth, your whimsy, your sadness, your frustration... you are worth it, and you are loved.

Gotta remember: we all are here on a visitor's pass.
Just like all these poems, I am a happy accident,
a series of improbable occurrences set up one after
another to bring me here and now. And so are you.
Welcome to the party, my friend.

POWER MINOR MAJOR MAYOR

HOIST WAIST WRIST

WHOLE BLOOM

GHOUL DRYER

&

GHOUL MAKES PASTE WASTE

SHAME GLUTE BRUTE

HOMER BUILD STACK TACKY

POLAR BEATS BAWDY

PROVE KNOWN

I love making books. I love Wordle.

This silly thing brings me joy. Thank you for being a part of it. If you would like to share in this journey, join the *if&when* Discord, where you can share your own found and curated poems, whether they are made of Wordle or anything else. This also is a space to keep track of upcoming poetry events, both virtually and in San Luis Obispo county, and eventually much more!

Join us at: www.ifwhen.us/discord

or here's a handy QR code:

Many thanks

I would like to thank Josh Wardle, the software engineer who created Wordle. I would also like to thank The New York Times Company, who acquired Wordle in January 2022 and still kept the game free while adding additional features and continuing the daily puzzles. Thanks to my wife, Nicole, for being a sounding board. Thanks to my mom, who loves my creativity when many others are baffled by it. Thanks to Chris Moody-Schulz, who invited me to read my poems accompanied by something — literally anything — at a poetry reading, and gave me the impetus to put this together. Thanks to my fellow poets and performers at that reading June 29th, 2025: Margaret Lange, Kathryn de Lancellotti, and Joan Gelfand.

About the author

Benjamin Daniel Lawless is a friend to people and poetry. He runs Penciled In, a book design and publishing company, and has designed over 70 books since 2005, including founding a 4 issue literary journal called *if&when.* He wrote two collections of poetry: *There is Nothing Poetic About Fish* (2008) and *The Last Spelling Bee* (2011). His third collection, *Everything Bubbles to the Surface* is due to be released once he takes a breath.

Made in the USA
Monee, IL
09 November 2026

67380382R10032